The Ice-Cream Factory

Contents

Annie Ortiz
Photographs by Anthony Hart

RIGBY

Our Class Visit

Do you ever wonder how some things are made? Our class wondered how ice cream, our favourite dessert, is made. So we made a trip to an ice-cream factory to find out!

These tanks hold 150,000 litres each!

Huge lorries bring milk from dairy farms to the factory. Workers pump the milk into big tanks.

Mixing Machines

The first machine heats
the milk to kill any germs.
We didn't know milk had
germs! Then another machine
mixes the heated milk until
it's smooth and thick.

80°C

Hot!

We wore hair
nets to keep the
factory clean!

The milk then goes into a blender like the ones we have at home – only much bigger! The blender is run by a computer.

Ingredients

← Each bag holds a tonne of sugar. The factory uses 10 to 12 bags a day.

The blender mixes cream and sugar with the milk. Mmm. Delicious!

Other Ingredients Can Include

eggs

fruit

nuts

They keep the flavouring in big jugs.

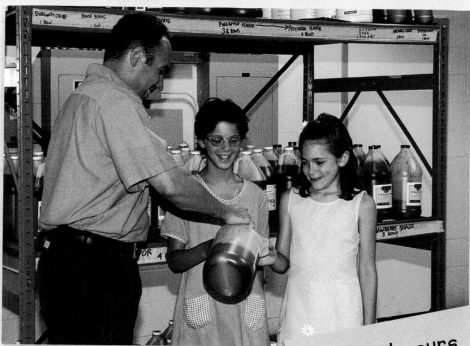

The factory makes two flavours of ice cream each day. Workers cut up fruit, like strawberries and peaches, to add to the ice cream.

Fruit Flavours

Strawberry

Peach

Banana

Cherry

Freezing

Then the ice cream goes through freezing pipes. The pipes are so cold that ice forms on them.

ice −7°C

Do not touch.

That makes the ice cream cold and soft. Yum!

Packing

Wear earplugs.
Too much noise.

Regular Flavours

Vanilla

Chocolate

Mint

Coffee

Lemon

In the packing area, the machines are very fast and VERY noisy. The workers have to wear earplugs. We had to wear earplugs too!

Watching the machines was fun.
One squirts the ice cream into cartons.

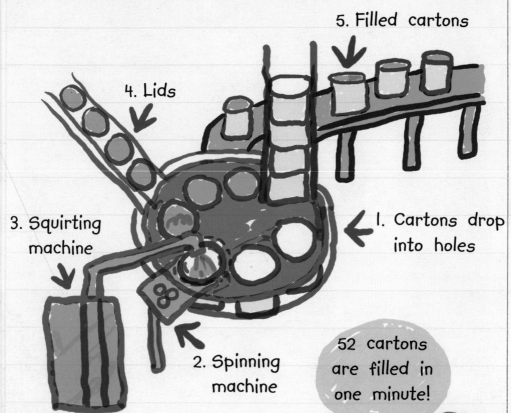

5. Filled cartons

4. Lids

3. Squirting machine

2. Spinning machine

1. Cartons drop into holes

52 cartons are filled in one minute!

Another spins the cartons round and round to get rid of air bubbles.

Hard Freezing

Finally, the ice cream is frozen solid in a very, very cold room. There is a machine that moves the air around. It is so cold it feels like 100° below zero in that room!

Cookie Flavours

Chocolate Chip

Cookies and Cream

Fudge Nut Brownie

Hot Fudge Brownie

11

Unusual Flavours

Ginger

Toffee Crunch

Tutti Frutti

Pistachio

It's so cold that the workers need to leave the freezer every 20 minutes to warm up. They can't wear contact lenses because they would stick to their eyes! Yuck! That's cold!

Shipping

Huge lorries take the ice cream to the shops. The trucks are like big freezers on wheels.

Flowchart

8. Lorries take ice cream to the shops.

1. Lorries bring milk to big tanks.

3. Cream and sugar are added and stirred.

2. Milk is heated and made smooth.

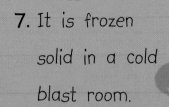

7. It is frozen solid in a cold blast room.

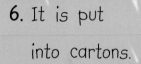

6. It is put into cartons.

4. Flavours are added.

5. The ice cream goes through freezing pipes.

Survey

We took a survey of
our favourite flavours.

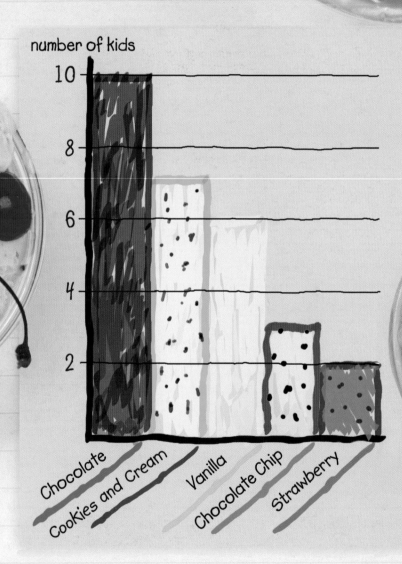

number of kids

10
8
6
4
2

Chocolate
Cookies and Cream
Vanilla
Chocolate Chip
Strawberry

What's your favourite ice cream?